You're in

Love

With a

Narcissist.

Alexandra Nouri

Copyright 2001-2012 Alexandra Nouri

All rights reserved. No part of this book may be used or reproduced in any manner whatsoever including posting on the Internet, without written permission of the author.

All personal quotes are used with permission.

Stonington Press

Vermont

...(T)he problem isn't that he needs more time or love, it's that you're working with extremely poor material. These guys have something wrong with them. And our goal is to get to a place where, when we hear that and know it's true, we say,

"Enough said."

--L.M.

I do not wish women to have power over men; but over themselves.

--Mary Wollstonecraft

...(I)mposed silence about any area of our lives is a tool for separation and powerlessness.

--Audre Lorde

A (Fore)Word About Gender

Most people with Narcissistic Personality Disorder are male. However, there certainly are female narcissists, and females with other personality disorders, and they are just as destructive to relationships as their male counterparts. If you have a female narcissist in your life, as you read please simply substitute pronouns as appropriate.

Contents

So. You're in Love With a Narcissist. Part 1   13

So. You're in Love With a Narcissist. Part 2   19

So. You're in Love With a Narcissist. Part 3   26

On All There Is to Know About Narcissists   31

Bonding With The Narcissist   37

The Devaluation Funhouse   41

The Narcissist as Editor-in-Chief   47

The Narcissist as Master Thespian   53

The Narcissist as Chubby Checker	59
Passion Aggression	63
You- You're Lea- You're Leaving The Narcissist?!	68
Missing The Narcissist	79

Further Reading

So.

You're in Love With a Narcissist.

Part 1

So, you're in love with a narcissist. That is SO cool; I'm guessing these are probably the best days of your life. Yeah, they have their foibles, but aren't they so emotionally satisfying, and just fun, fun, fun?

Good Lord.

Let's peek at some traits.

"Usually above-average intelligence..." Compared to what? They have abilities and can perform necessary tasks just like any other psychopathic lunatic, I'll give them that. But these people are the stupidest people on Earth. There is ZERO depth to their awareness.

Take your last conversation with him (permit me the traditional pronoun here, please, gender-aware reader). Did you come away feeling enlightened? Enriched? Like you'd 'shared?' Or like you'd just tried to speak with a drunken baboon vaunting an attitude problem? Was it a mutually beneficial exchange of ideas, opinions or feelings, or was it you being sane and trying to make the simplest of points and him copping a defensive stance that would make the Iraqi Army jealous, using doublespeak and laughable (if they weren't so ugly) non sequiturs designed to flummox you and make him look victorious?

IQ aside, only a moron would take a clear statement such as, "You contradicted yourself, and I need to know what you really meant," and internally process it thusly: 'RED ALERT! RED ALERT! Attack! Assault! Oh, so I'm contradicting myself, eh? You think I'm just a contradicting, know-nothing, argumentative horse turd, eh? You think I'm just a worthless dumb-ass jerk, eh? Well, I'll show you! I'LL GET YOU FOR THAT!'

Look at him with love and devotion and say, "I need to know what you mean when you say, 'This relationship is a side-track event.' Do you understand?" He'll look like a deer caught in your headlights, and then collect himself and say, "Of course I understand. You're confused by facts and logic."

Hm. Brainy.

"Seeks out adulation..." Here's where some of us trip up. We love giving love, and love it when it's well-received. Here's the fact of it: It ain't love they want. Love is deep. Narcissists have the depth of a sidewalk mud puddle. They only want love to the extent that it looks like worship. They like, "Oh, I just loved the way you parked the car. How do you do that, always so straight and just the right distance from the house (moonstruck looks, starry eyes)?" They hate, "I love you, and I was wondering if you thought about the future." Even if that's presented after 12 years together, you're on a romantic boat trip and you're pregnant, it will be processed thusly: "RED ALERT! RED ALERT! Assault! Attack! You want to rip away my freedom, eh? Tell me what to do, eh? You think I can just be your puppet? You think YOU should be the one to make these decisions? Well, I'LL GET YOU FOR THAT!"

And they do. Oh, they do.

So:

You're in Love With a

Narcissist.

Part 2

Any more traits lying around here?

"Exploitive..." Oh, ignore that. It sounds so negative. They don't 'exploit,' per se, they just... 'enjoy and don't bother reciprocating.'

Let's say you're seeing a dashing, sensitive narcissist. You meet at the beach, have a picnic that you brought, you listen to his bitching and tell him what a masterful work of art he is; you walk back to your house, you make love; he naps, gets up and showers, and, with a kiss, of course, leaves and you don't hear from him for a week. A normal guy might call, send flowers, ask you out the next night, take you to meet his friends, something boring like that. But a narcissist, he's got things to do! People to see! PRIORITIES! If you say, "I need to see you more. I feel like you don't take us seriously," he'll probably respond with a reassuring and comforting selection from the following, meant to end the discussion cold:

"I know. This is hard."

"I just don't know if I can."

"Maybe you just need to decide what we have is enough."

"But this is special. Like a summertime affair. We're like kids again."

"I do take it seriously. It just doesn't seem that way to you. Maybe something's wrong with you."

"Sense of entitlement..." Well, yes. When he's the most special, unique butthole in existence, he has certain perks. One is that he gets to do whatever he wants, to whomever he wants, right at that moment. This is particularly so as applied to you, the one who loves him. He gets to flirt and not have it bother you. He gets to ignore you and have you gush with joy when you see him next, like some codependent Irish Setter. He gets to tell you it's over and dump you and then come back to your open arms when he's short on attention from other people. And, most of all, he gets to soak up the attention you give him, bask in it, and then sneer at you and go get more from someone else.

Now, some of these "medical criteria" can be a little vague; let's see if we can be a little more experience-based about it:

If the most sensitive thing he's said in six months is, "Your sister's really beautiful," or, "I mean, she's REALLY beautiful," he might be a narcissist.

If he's so fake that professional actors walk away from him weeping openly with feelings of inadequacy, he might be a narcissist.

If the only time he gives you a gift of any substance is when he wants something from you or he thinks it will impress other people, he might be a narcissist.

If his idea of a close, intimate evening involves his telling you in front of a fireplace that he might be in love with someone else, or getting up and leaving early because he has "things he has to do," and he drops these stink-bombs so often that you've come to expect them, he might be a narcissist.

If after sex you have the vague, persistent feeling that you should have been paid for what just took place, he might be a narcissist.

If he's sitting at a funeral service and he whispers to you, "Aren't they going to have SOME kind of entertainment?", he might be a narcissist.

If he broke it off with you, sucked you back in, broke it off with you, sucked you back in, broke it off with you, and, when you resisted his sucking you back in he

REALLY turned on the charm and pushed all your buttons and did everything humanly possible to suck you back in until you caved and you were sucked back in, and then he broke it off with you, he's very probably a narcissist.

If within ten hours after your wedding he undergoes a shift that would make Dr. Jekyl jealous and acts like he can't stand being with you, a demeanor that hangs around in varying degrees for the rest of your relationship, he's very probably a narcissist.

And if he acts like a warm, devoted, responsive partner when other people are looking, and then literally drops his arm from around your shoulders after they've left and, when you try to elicit more attention from him, he blocks you, he's definitely a narcissist.

If your narcissist throws you a crumb of attention, take it and savor it and deluge him with appreciation for it. Do NOT under ANY circumstances snort with disgust and drop his sorry ass to free yourself up for someone much, much better. Hang onto him at all costs. ALL COSTS. This won't do you a damn bit of good, but it will help keep him away from the rest of us.

So, You're in Love With a Narcissist.

Part 3

OK. On a less acerbic note.

Now, we know love is a good thing. Good love involves exchanging respect, affection, time and support with someone special. It feels good and when it has rough spots the two parties work them through.

But the harsh truth is that there are those among us who don't love. And when they pretend to, at our expense, that's a painful thing for the rest of us. They pretend to love because they know we'll love them back and they like the way it feels when we adore them and struggle to make a relationship with them work. It makes them feel special.

But one day we look up and we see that we're the one putting in all the respect, affection, time and support, and they're taking it as well-deserved worship and hold out their hands for more.

We try to work through rough spots. And with a narcissist that's where the REAL ouchies kick in.

...od people look at the matter and review ... as well as that of their partner.

...arcissists are so desperate to always look perfect to themselves that the chances are zero of them ever considering they might have caused someone discomfort. So, if the two of you have a problem, guess whose fault it is?

In rough spots, good people look toward the goal of working it out and going on in better understanding. Narcissists would rather dump the whole thing and start fresh with someone else. If you're with a narcissist, your purpose in life is to reassure them that they're as perfect as they want to be. So, if you find that there's something imperfect about them and show it, as in your saying, "You hurt my feelings," "But you said you'd call. I needed to hear from you," or "Why did you spend our whole night at the party talking to the pretty woman from work?", then you aren't doing your job and may need to be replaced with someone much weaker or more troubled. (Healthy, strong people defend their due and their boundaries in relationships. Narcissists hate that.)

In rough spots, good people engage in logical though maybe passionate debates about the issues. They ask each other what they want and use that information to make each other and themselves happy and fulfilled. A narcissist may very well ask you what you want; they'll then use that information to manipulate you by threatening to withhold what you need and try to extract more attention and reassurance from you. And this is what you'll get in return: punishment for having challenged their perfection in the first place. Threats of abandonment. Accusations. Contempt.

Does all this sound far-fetched and like a lame made-for-TV movie? Then you've never had an encounter with a narcissist.

If you're with a narcissist, do research. Write your feelings down. Get some therapy. Do whatever helps, but before you do anything, get out. Just get out. And don't look back. The view isn't pretty.

On All There Is to Know

About Narcissists

First, a given: Yes, you should research all you can about NPD. Knowledge is power; knowledge is good.

But. Until you're out, I'll defend all research that empowers you to get out, and no more.

The harsh truth about their recovery: Inside their heads is such a maelstrom of negativity and abject disturbance that it's best to just write them off as totaled and shop for a new model.

If you start wondering too hard about what makes him tick in hopes of understanding them better and working with him, you're tiptoeing into a minefield: Because you're a loving soul devoted to your man, you're going to be looking for some loophole, some soft spot or workable aspect to his disturbance and identify that as a way that you can help him or stay with him. "Ah! He wasn't born that way, so I can help him get over the trauma of his childhood!" "Look, he's just in his avoidance phase of the classic approach/avoidance conflict right now. He'll come around." "He's just anxious that I'll abandon him, that's why he's being manipulative and threatening right now. He just needs my love."

Boom.

OK, so if you insist on wondering and researching the mechanics of their behaviors, at least keep all this in mind:

Point 1) Narcissism IS their personality. It's locked firmly in place. It's going nowhere. It's not like a tumor that can be excised. It's systemic and permanent, a part of them, like Down's Syndrome or being tall. Whether they were born that way or got that way later doesn't matter for you; they are that way, forever.

Point 2) Challenging them with reason or healthy indignation when they're nasty will fail; they'll combat you into defeat at all costs. Your "going with the flow" when they're nasty will fail; it may get you through the conflict at hand, but repeated application will result in their getting bored and punishing you for "not caring enough to work on this," AND you'll grow numb and weak with complacency and resignation. There is no successful maneuver for working with narcissists. You'll lose every time.

Point 3) The pain of the abuses at the hands of someone who was born a narcissist is exactly as painful as those of someone who became one in childhood. The abuse caused by a narcissist whose mother tragically abandoned them in infancy is just as cold and hurtful as that of any other psychopath. Whether they're born or made; whether they're classified just right in the DSM or not; whether they're 'mentally ill' or 'emotionally ill;' whether they're severe NPD, 'narcissistic type' or "only" have 'narcissistic tendencies,' doesn't matter here. Leave all that to the university guys. Study it yourself after you're out and away and he's leaving you alone. The abuse hurts you deep and hard no matter what labels and qualifiers are slapped on the narcissist. Try all the maneuvers you want, but if he's close to you, if you're in contact with him, he'll hurt you.

Research away, but never forget that the reason you're looking into NPD is because you've been emotionally devastated at the hands of a psychopath. Start feeling sorry for them or thinking that there's some hope and you've not only shifted accountability for their abuse away from them, but you've given yourself a reason to keep at it. To stay. To love him more and try harder.

Boom.

Bonding With the Narcissist

Would you like to bond with a narcissist?

Would you like a talking frog with that?

The talking frog is more likely.

Narcissists don't bond. Which is why they make such horrific parents. Imagine being a baby, or two, or four or ten years old, and having your intermediary with the rest of the huge scary world, your only source of security and love, be a fake, detached, disordered shell of a person who pushes you away when you hold your arms up to them, and arbitrarily thrashes between open contempt and ignoring you throughout your childhood. (Hopefully you are "imagining" it and not "remembering" it.)

Now, they can fake it, mind you. And they do. But that gets tiring, and because it's all an act it can be very exhausting and bring on resentment that they need to do this lame-ass "bonding" thing at all beyond the first days or weeks of knowing you.

One of the more obvious character traits of the narcissist is his uncanny selfishness. An almost unbelievable grade of selfishness. He's a caricature of selfishness. So focused is he on his needs and wants that taking yours seriously is quite out of the question. He'll even neglect or completely ignore basic bonding behaviors (affection, warm conversation, intimacy) that will help keep your attention and reassurance flowing his way, not only because he thinks you should give those things to him without his having to do or say anything, but also because bonding behaviors don't even occur to him. The bonding part of his brain has curdled down to nothing.

The bonding part of his heart is a big empty hole.

Sad, yes, but not your fault, not your responsibility and not fixable. Whatever it is about the narcissist in your life that you like, you will find it in someone else who does not have a disturbance and who can bond. You deserve that by virtue of your being alive and well. Throwing your efforts away on a narcissist is as pointless as looking for the talking frog.

Ribbitt.

The Devaluation Funhouse

So, you still hanging on to that narcissist? Good for you! I know, he's beaten your soul out of recognition and you don't know who you are anymore, but hang in there, things might turn around someday!

By now you're great friends with an adorable little quirk called devaluation. As you know, just about anything can bring this scene on, such as he'd had salami for lunch, you asked him if anything was wrong, his friend got a new girlfriend, or you were so out of control as to criticize him (such as, "I feel like I'm not as important to you as I used to be," or, "It was manipulative of you to threaten to leave if I didn't do as you say"). The mind of the narcissist is wildly chaotic, fraught with conflicts and about as predictable as the bullets in Russian Roulette.

But, usually, here's what happened: You Two Got Too Close. Yes, you probably invoked that bane of narcissistic existence, Mister Intimacy. Cuddling after nookie, kissing anytime outside of foreplay (when he initiates it), talk of meaningful growth in the relationship such as a commitment (even if he's living in your house and you've been together five years) or spending time with other couples-- though this is all pleasurable and welcomed by good men, you were a very bad girl for subjecting your poor narcissist to such torture.

And here's how you're punished. At the drop of a hat, and usually after a particularly reassuring and close time together, he'll insult you. Or threaten the relationship. He'll tell you he doesn't see how the two of you will make it. You're so demanding. Projection is common: You don't give him what he needs. You play mind games with him. You. You. You.

Now, this serves a gleefully vast array of purposes. One, it puts distance between the two of you and abates that terrifying and nauseatingly moist intimacy you two had going. Two, it makes you anxious and upset, and as all good narcissists know, how much they can hurt you is an EXCELLENT indicator of how important they are to you. Three, you immediately begin to try to reason with him or find out what brought this on, and that, of course, is rich, full-bodied attention directed at him, the nectar of narcissistic life. Four, you might threaten to leave him, which in his absolutely chaotic and absurd mind is what he wants, as a latent response to childhood anxieties. (Go ahead and convincingly say you're leaving. Watch him shift into capitulation overdrive. You'll see a turn-around that'll make your head spin.)

The most common form of narcissistic devaluation is the blame-and-bolt maneuver. You two are doing great. You're sitting on the porch together, playing footsies, talking about the dog. Then, he drops a dig.

"If we break up, I think you should take the dog."

This comes out of nowhere. You catch your breath and say, "What do you mean? Why would we break up?"

"Well," his powerful logic informs you, "Like I've said before, I just don't know if this can work out."

"But, it already is working out. Why wouldn't it work

out?"

"I don't know," he shrugs. "I just never really know with you. Sometimes I feel like you'd rather die than let me know what you're thinking. I don't think a relationship can survive like that."

You sit in stunned silence, remembering his complaining the day before that you talked too much.

"So," he concludes with a flourish, "I don't know. That's all I can say. I just don't know." And, if he's bored with your response because it's not riveting or desperate enough: "I gotta go."

SCORE!! You've been devalued! Sadistically put down, robbed of any orientation or security, told you're disposable, and it's ALL YOUR FAULT. Optional ornaments include rage, obscenity, name-calling, and maybe even a clichéd insult or two. (Narcissists aren't the most creative psychopaths in the DSM.)

If you're with a man who devalues you just once, get out. If you give him another chance, the probability of him doing it again and again is 100%. Your love and efforts will not save the relationship, it will bring on more devaluation. Get out and find somebody sane.

The Narcissist as

Editor-in-Chief

Ever wonder how the narcissist you know can live with himself? Well, the best weapon in his self-love arsenal is something I like to call Selective Editing.

The narcissist edits the past. He edits the present. He'll tell himself things are exactly the way they need to be for him to have an unblemished, sterling image of himself, even if that involves saying you started an argument when you hadn't even opened your mouth, or saying he was hurt that you avoided him yesterday when actually he'd told you a week ago he needed a break from you and not to call, or telling you he loves going out with you and that he loved the opera when the fact is he bitched about the opera from before you left until long after you got home. All with a straight face, a level eye and sometimes a clenched jaw.

If the two of you have a conflict, he'll tweak the facts as much as he has to in order to make it all your fault. He'll tell you how you feel and if, later in the day, he needs you to have felt different, he'll tweak it again. He shapeshifts to suit his mood (remember the roiling chaos in his head?) and to appear the star of any moment, and any tiny or not-so-tiny adjustments to the facts that need to be made for him to be the star are fine. The facts are incidental. Your feelings are of no import. What truly counts is his thinking he's perfect.

Some people call this "lying," but there is actually a nuance of a difference in that as the words are leaving his mouth the narcissist actually believes what he's saying. He not only thinks it's true, he'll defend it to the death.

Until he forgets it twenty seconds later.

Then, whatever is leaving his mouth THEN is the inviolable truth.

If he contradicts himself? Point this out to him. Some of the best narcissist lines ever uttered can come next.

"I know it can seem that way sometimes to you. It's inevitable."

"You weren't listening the first time."

"Not at all. Both are true, just in different ways."

"I don't have to be consistent to be right. Everyone knows that."

"What, are you calling me a liar? Aren't you projecting a little here?"

One can only watch in speechless wonder as the narcissist, endowed with the powers of the Great and Wonderful Oz, knits and weaves such fanciful fiction, such utter animal excrement, out of nowhere to "explain" his behavior, mood or inclination of the moment. If he needs you to have been inexplicably distant in the recent past, you were. If he needs to have been gushingly attentive while you were so distant, he was. He'll take the tiniest, most unrelated detail and inflate it into an event of such import as to direct the rest of your future together. He'll take a response on your part to his selfishness or manipulation (You: "I'm sorry, but if you're going to always pull away from me like this when I need you the most, then I think we need to reassess our relationship"), and create a story around it that has him the victim of your senseless wrath, your fickle and arbitrary abuse. (Him, later, about the words above: "Like that time you broke us up-- and, I'd like you to admit you did break us up-- because of your unrealistic expectations of me, and blindsiding me when I needed you the most?")

Reality is highly malleable in Narcissist World. What can't be messed with is his pathological idea of his own unique perfection. And he needs YOU to reassure him of that perfection with a never-ending flow of attention, adoration and praise. If you're hopelessly stuck in reality like the boring boorish masses (that is, good, cool people with no psychiatric disorders to hide) and can't spend your life in his world where it's a privilege to help distort the truth to accommodate his self-image and worship his magnificent being, then there's going to be a problem.

The Narcissist as

Master Thespian

All you idealistic young (i.e. younger than 30) whippersnappers out there might not remember this, but Jon Lovitz used to have a character on Saturday Night Live called the Master Thespian. He was a caricature of a stage actor backstage, in a silk robe and scarf, with pompous gestures and a hilariously dramatic voice. He'd act out "rage" or "anguish," and his fellow thespian, being understandably fooled and taking him oh so seriously, would try to assuage him. Here, Master Thespian would say:

"Acting!"

His friend would cry, "Brilliant!"

Master Thespian would reply, "Thank You!"

Which brings us to your cuddly life partner, the narcissist. (You ARE still with him, aren't you? You PROMISED to keep him, don't forget. That way he only annoys the rest of us by flirting with us unrelentingly and making us gag with his pomposity, rather than his actually putting us at risk by pursuing us.)

No actor on earth is more the master thespian than the narcissist. Actors take breaks. Not so the narcissist. He is ALWAYS acting. His whole life is pretend. This is one of the biggest cues to most people that the narcissist has something weird and creepy about him; he can't help but show himself as ridiculously and somewhat nauseatingly fake. He seems shallow and untrustworthy in his fakery. He seems that way because he is that way.

He feels exceedingly comfortable fantasizing because it feels like real life to him; nice, comfy and familiar. He spends a lot of time fantasizing because real life tends to let him down a lot, since all the stupid boors around him fail to see him for his true worth, and in fantasy he can revel in the worship that is his due. The trouble is, his actual presentation is so fake that it gets all mixed up with his fantasies, and so here is one thing the narcissist will never, ever say:

"Acting!"

In fact, if you EVER suggest he's faking or playing up anything, chances are he'll turn on you like a rabid jackal and hate your guts the rest of your life. His image of perfection means that he must be seen as authentic and credible, and that the perfect shell he projects is perfectly believable every moment. He'll tell you you're projecting, cruel, off-topic and totally wrong. And that HE is REAL.

This is part of the reason why nothing they say means anything. Mostly it's because they're forever editing their reality, and if one minute he's going to marry you and asks you to pick out the house, he'll likely say the opposite soon afterwards and deny ever even suggesting such a thing. But another reason you can't possibly take these guys seriously is because their whole life is a charade, a drama being read from an ever-changing script. There's no foundation of meaning or depth of character to anything they say or do, no continuity or rhythm at all. They are truly a thin veneer of plastic personality covering an empty interior. When he seems to love you, he's faking. When he appears to want to get closer to you, he's acting. He's not "exaggerating true feelings" or "especially passionate," he's faking. It's all an act designed to get you to feed him attention and adoration. Yes, it really is that sick. And yes, he'll always devalue you in the end. Every single time.

Ah, the stimulating challenge of it! You are one lucky mama-- you get to play daily head games and you keep your mind sharp by second-guessing every single thing out of his mouth, AND you get drama, you get theater, you get play-acting that, admittedly, isn't even remotely entertaining, but is all his disturbed personality can muster.

Whoops, there comes your man the narcissist.

Lights.

Camera.

ACTION!

The Narcissist as

Chubby Checker

"Come on Baby!" Chubby Checker coaxed a generation. "Let's do the twist!"

And the narcissist, ever the eager beaver, does The Twist in spades. The narcissist twists everything. Words. Intentions. Facts. Nothing is too self-evident or too important to be twisted and contorted out of recognition by the narcissist to suit his agenda of the moment.

Did you tell him you won't sleep with him as long as he

has a girlfriend? "Well, it looks like we can't see each other anymore, because of these religious issues you have."

Did you tell him you don't like it when he flirts with every woman in sight? "What, all this fuss because I asked Jennifer how she is? I see you and she must have a personality conflict."

Did you have to leave his place early once about three weeks earlier to go pick up your kids or make sure your sick aunt got some dinner? "Well, maybe we should rethink this involvement. Your priorities don't seem to include a relationship right now." (This also features a favorite NPD tool called "projection.")

Did you tell him it was rude for him to keep you waiting two hours while he sat shooting the breeze with the guys after work? "Boy, this really is a zero-sum game with you, isn't it? Isn't what we have more solid than that?"

Which brings us to an important point about the narcissist's doing The Twist: It doesn't even have to make any sense, as long as he feels like he's squirmed out of being busted right at that second. If he can leave you vaguely stunned by how utterly absurd his response is, in his chaotic mind that's just as satisfying as a "win" as actually being right. Does it sometimes seem like he pulls this stuff out of thin air just to look victorious? That's because that's exactly what he's doing.

So, the next time that narcissist starts distorting what you say and do to make him feel smart and like he's got you and the situation controlled, just picture him as he really is: frantically, desperately, and very poorly doing The

Twist as Chubby Checker NEVER intended it to be done.

Passion Aggression

Take the word passion. Split it up, add a handful of letters, and you get passive aggression!

Coincidence? I think not!

Narcissists have to feel like you think they're supremely and exquisitely perfect, all of the time. (If you fail in making them feel that way, the problem is with you, not them.) They also need to punish you for slights such as wanting them to be honest and direct with you, and they devalue you so that you don't threaten them with intimacy and healthy expectations. One wouldn't think they could accomplish both being perfect and being punishing and devaluing at the same time, but they're damn well going to try. What ensues is passive aggression.

Narcissists love passive aggression because they get to be cruel, sadistic and punishing without having it overtly look that way. They can pull nasty stunts and have it look like an accident or like the responsibility of someone else, most likely you. They love being "late" for dates and appointments with you. They love telling you they'll do something and then saying later that you misunderstood. They really love sniveling little digs like, "Last night with you was fun. You were hardly critical or nagging at all."

The most prevalent passion you're going to get from the narcissist, far more than romantic passion and even more yet than passion for life, is passive aggression. Narcissists throw great energy and practice into their passive aggression. As a result they're good at it, though not usually very subtle.

His favorite passive aggressive move will be ignoring you. Days without word from him, if you're dating; days without touching you or talking to you in complete sentences, if you're living with him.

If something is important to you or hard for you, he'll minimize it and turn your attention to himself. If your mother is terminally ill or you just found out you can't have children, he'll manage to be away from you for long periods of time and when he's with you he'll talk about the biggest issue in his own life, usually something like the fungus on his toenail or how his boss snubbed him that day.

If you're laying in bed weak with the flu and have four or five kids galloping around needing parenting, he'll go ahead and knock off work early on Friday and go on a four-hour kayaking trip with a couple (predominantly female) friends. Then he'll call you from the parking lot on the way home and ask if he can pick you up some soda crackers or something, and expect to be showered with appreciation and await your tears of joy at having someone so deeply considerate as he. When you fail to do so, it will be YOU and your COLD, unloving self that is responsible for any ensuing tension.

And tension there will be, if you persist in your irrational assaults of pointing out his behavior. PLAY ALONG, DAMMIT!! He'll be giving you a chance to make up for your lack of appreciation, your attacks on his very being, your being sick in the first place; APOLOGIZE! Then the passive aggression can eventually subside.

People with prolonged exposure to narcissists need intensive therapy. They're often on anti-depressant medication and have health problems like migraines and Chronic Fatigue Syndrome. They've forgotten their purpose in life and they feel numb. They can have symptoms of Post Traumatic Stress Disorder or Prolonged Duress Stress Disorder.

Coincidence?

I think not.

You-

You're Lea-

You're Leaving The

Narcissist?!

So.

I hear you're beginning to consider thinking about mulling over the possibility of your perhaps pulling away from that narcissist of yours.

WHY??!! Why unleash his toxic spewing on the rest of us; why grasp at the vision of a happy and fulfilling life for yourself while making the rest of us targets for his fake, psychopathic pursuits?

AFTER ALL I'VE DONE FOR YOU??!!

All right. If you're going to continue with this infuriatingly healthy, sane line of thinking, there are some things you should know.

**Narcissists HATE to lose. When you say, "It's over," you, a sane person, mean, "It's over." To the psycho you're talking to, however, you are throwing down the gauntlet and saying, "Take THAT, Buttface." If you say it's over, he'll instantly click into "I don't think so" mode. Which brings us to:

**He WILL pursue victory. He won't pursue YOU. It will LOOK like he's pursuing you, but I assure you most vigorously, he's not. He's wanting to put things right back to the way they're SUPPOSED to be, with him screwing with your mind and your taking it, with your dousing him with adoration and admiration no matter how he treats you, and if you take him back he WILL incorporate in there some punishment for your "abandoning" him. He wants you back, all right, but on his terms, with exactly the same degree of selfishness and psychopathy as before. Nothing has changed. If you respond to him and give him another chance, you'll regret it.

**He will want to check up on you. Because he loves you? Oh, my, you haven't been listening, have you. No, because he wants to make sure you're suffering without him. Memorize this: Knowing you're miserable without him is as satisfying to him as having you with him. If he can't keep you feeding him attention in the relationship, he wants to know that you're thinking of him and having a hard time without him afterwards. He'll eventually offer to alleviate your suffering by accepting any and all apologies and taking you back, and then once you're together again he'll abuse you until you get sick of it and end it again. If he can keep you swaying nauseatingly between the two situations indefinitely, he will be having a very happy time of it indeed.

**Your only hope for success is a cold turkey break-up. No, you can't "still be friends." No, the occasional e-mail is not harmless. Narcissists who have been dumped will NOT be normal ex-mates any more than they were normal mates. Respond to him and he will, without fail, hurt you and devalue you again. Every little contact, every "chance encounter," will set you back in recovering from what's been a psychologically traumatic experience for you. You can't heal from a trauma you're still experiencing. If you're going to recover from this, you MUST stay away from him. Marvel from a distance at his efforts to hurt and abuse you even though you're not even together anymore.

There are a couple of different strains of narcissistic ex-mates.

The Herpes Narcissist ~ He never goes away completely and flares up when you need it the least. He will come back and act like absolutely nothing has happened and the two of you were just having a tiny tiff, for which he's prepared to forgive you. He'll act this way even though you've been ignoring him for four months and have a restraining order out on him. This looks like love and devotion on his part, but it's not. If you warm to him in a weak moment he'll do a brilliant job of reminding you why you left him in the first place, and you'll have suffered a major setback.

The Lyme Disease Narcissist ~ He goes away, but not until you've employed radical defense routines for months and then you're left with bothersome lasting reminders of the experience. If you were married and have kids together, he'll make your divorce proceedings a living hell just like he did your marriage. He'll act like he can't wait to get rid of you, and then stall and impede the divorce as much as humanly possible just to make sure you know who's in control. And that's BEFORE the real nightmare begins, with the custody arrangements. You need to stay as strong as a pillar of rock to get through it, and then you still have to deal with him until the kids are grown.

The Itchy Rash Narcissist ~ The best of the four, really. The only way to get over an itchy rash is to ignore it no matter how excruciatingly annoying it is, no matter how much you know giving it attention with bring relief, and then after ages of depriving it of attention it really does go away.

A very few lucky targets (as target luck goes) are dealing with a **Train Wreck Narcissist**. This variety is very rare; I've only heard of a scant few. These jewels will, often without warning or provocation, leave suddenly and completely with as much cruelty and abuse as possible and are never heard from again. Often they will sniff a hint of intent on your part to end or at least abate the abuse you're enduring, and in a knee-jerk response they'll do what they perceive to be abandoning you before you abandon them, and they'll do it coldly, harshly and totally. Though their targets are devastated and profoundly hurt, they are left alone to commence their recovery without threat of interference from the abuser. They don't feel even remotely lucky, and I have utter compassion for that, but in the context of recovering targets, they're sitting prettier than they'll ever know – because they can recover in peace.

The best way to get rid of a narcissistic tumor on your life is to "stay down" in his eyes when he's in his devalue-you stage. It's like a head start on a new life without his crap. He'll probably ignore you and treat you like dirt, and then, later, want to see you again. Here's where you ignore him. Treat him as you would the unfortunate young man two doors down who has a man's body but the wits of a four-year-old, and who knows how to dial your number and send e-mails but who has absolutely nothing to say. Just likes doing it. Get caller ID and don't answer his calls. Delete messages without reading them. If he shows up, keep the conversation on the doorstep-- don't let him in. Just answer with bland monosyllabic responses, no questions. They HATE to be thought of as boring; if that's the vibe he gets from you, he'll fade away comparatively quickly.

Trust me. This is what you want.

All narcissists are selfish, mentally disturbed abusers. They're not cute, they're not cuddly, and they don't have "hidden potential." They don't "get better." They're self-absorbed actors pretending whatever they have to in order to get attention. Period. Hear the fat lady singing?

After an experience with a narcissist, you'll need to recover. You've been badly used and abused, and you need to face that in order to go on and have a healthy, whole life. You need to mourn and you need to get mad about how that bustard had the nads to hurt you like that, before you can heal. Remember: Every word, glimpse or gesture from or about him is a trigger, a set-back, and the fewer of these you allow into your life, the faster and cleaner your recovery will be.

Missing the Narcissist

Now you've done it. Forced to choose between your own sanity, your future and sense of self, and the arbitrary, absurdly selfish whims of a mentally ill manipulator, you've chosen the high road to peace and clear thinking. You've broken up with the narcissist.

IT'S NOT TOO LATE!!!! CALL HIM!!! Beg his forgiveness! Yes, he'll wiggle with glee at your showering him with this attention and taunt you with ambivalence or outright haughty insults as punishment for your taking control of your own life, but hang in there! You might still be able to resume your place in his whacked psychoworld!

OK. I know. You miss him. We all know how that feels. But, now, let's take a peek at this 'missing' thing.

I assume we all agree that with narcissists, we're generally dealing with two people: The guy he is, and the guy he pretended to be. You miss one of them. I take it we all know which one.

Pretend Guy is gone. Deceased. This hurts. This really hurts. It needs to be mourned. In addition to the loss of Pretend Guy, you've got mucho grande abuses heaped on you by Actual Guy. Topping off this pile of misery and trauma, Actual Guy and Pretend Guy inhabit the same body. Only another psycho wouldn't be thrown into a tailspin by the surrealism of it all.

When he calls you after the breakup, he sounds just like Pretend Guy! 'You're alive!,' you think. 'You're not dead! Yes, YOU are my true love! You're finally back! Oh, WHEN can I see you?'

Whoa, there, Sister. Let me spare you a tiny bit of hurt here by having us skip ahead to where he slams you again and you wake up in the harsh, cold world of Reality. Things just got even worse. Pretend Guy is still gone, Actual Guy is still abusing you, Pretend Guy and Actual Guy are still the same guy, AND now any baby steps into healing you might have made just got deleted into nothingness.

And you wonder how he's feeling. Of course you do; not only are you sensitive and caring (narcissists don't pick hardasses for partners), but also you're conditioned to feel that way. The entire relationship was about him and his wants and needs. He literally trained you to think of little else. The real you, the pre-narcissist you, doesn't want an abusive, mentally ill, inconsistent, selfish freak, ridiculous in his pandering for attention, chock full of contempt and inner conflicts that spill out and burn you. The real you wants a real partner.

"Hey," I hear one loyal heroine say. "Don't talk about him like that! He's NOT an abusive, selfish freak! He's.... Well, OK, he's an abusive, inconsistent, selfish, ridiculous, freak, but he's MY abusive, selfish freak!" Oh. Sorry. Hey, didn't I see you last week on Jerry Springer?

For the rest of us, we need to heed the experiences of my online friend Lin. Lin's man came on strong. Charming.

Wonderful. They married, and he immediately became selfish, cold, and ambivalent about their marriage but refused to leave; he was unempathic, wildly defensive and manipulative. He was a Narcissist. Lin knew something was morbidly wrong, but she stayed; he'd grow distant, she'd work to make it better. How long did this go on before she read the writing on the wall?

Friend Lin stayed with her narcissist for three decades, until she 'selfishly' left him to preserve the remaining shards of sanity she had. I wonder if she has any regrets about leaving and wishes she could have him back, or if she has any general advice for the rest of us. Let's ask her, shall we?

Alex: Hey, Lin. Do you have any advice for the gals out here who are on the fence about their narcissist partners?

Lin: G E T! O U T! I WENT THROUGH YEARS OF HELL. I SHOULD HAVE LEFT THIRTY YEARS AGO. I WANT MY THIRTY YEARS BACK!!!

Hmmm. Well, don't pay any attention to her. She should have stayed for 31 years; maybe THEN he would have changed. Besides, YOUR narcissist is different! HE'LL get better! He will! I swear! Please, just take him back and get him away from the rest of us...

When we leave the narcissist, it's because the abuse has gotten intolerable. Afterward, when he calls us and pushes the buttons he knows extremely well, the temptation to give him another chance can be overwhelming. We're hurt; we're mad; we want to recoup some of our losses; we love him and want it to work; we just can't believe that anyone would be so warped as to hurt us that way, so we want to give them the benefit of the doubt. All roads point to trying again with the narcissist.

Except for one. Reality. Truth. Knowledge, and honesty with yourself. Your peace. Your health. This road points in the opposite direction away from the narcissist. Yes, it's an uphill road, but if you can invest in the climb the view from the top is spectacular.

Does it seem like if you just invested enough love and time in the narcissist, well, it just can't help but to get better?

Our Lin spent 30 years wanting her narcissist to get better. I wonder if he started to get a little better around year 10. Or year 17. Year 23? Year 29? Is L. content that she tried hard enough to make the relationship work?

85

Let's ask Lin.

Alex: Hey, Lin, are you glad you spent 30 years in a 'relationship' with a narcissist?

Lin: AAUUUUUGGGGGGHHHH.......

AAAAAAACCCCCCKKKKHHHHHH....

Sorry, folks. Apparently I said something wrong.

With toxic men, relationships without boundaries are downright dangerous. You lose yourself in his reality, and his reality is a distorted, self-centered one.

--Joseph W. Rock, Psy.D and Barry L. Duncan, Psy.D.

Though no one can go back and make a brand new start, anyone can start from now and make a brand new ending.

--Carl Bard

... Controllers are shocked if the relationship ends. They not only don't know that they are pretending, they don't know that their ignorance predisposes them to mind-boggling behaviors. Their idea of themselves as "wonderful" blinds them to the impact of their behavior -- reactions to, and defenses against, all threats to their illusory connection. They are difficult to deal with at best. They are terrifying and life-threatening at worst.

--Patricia Evans

[The narcissist] is a ... master at frustrating others - frustrating their small and big hopes, their need for attention, reassurance, time, company, enjoyment. When others remonstrate against such treatment, [he tells himself] it is their neurotic sensitivity that makes them react this way.

--Karen Horney MD

What you are will show in what you do.

--Thomas A. Edison

[The narcissist] may be extremely proud, consciously or unconsciously, of his faculty of fooling everybody -- and in his arrogance and contempt for others believes that he actually succeeds in this.

--Karen Horney MD

...[T]hose with personality disorders perceive the world as a much more threatening place than most people do. Therefore, their perceptions of other people's behavior is often distorted -- and in some cases delusional. ... They may form very inaccurate beliefs about the other person, but cling rigidly to those beliefs when they are challenged -- because being challenged is usually perceived as a threat.

--William A. Eddy, LCSW, Esq.

As far as the narcissist is concerned, there is only one point of view, [his] own.

--William S. Hamrick

Further Reading

Horney, Karen MD: Neurosis and Human Growth - The Struggle Toward Self-Realization. W.W. Norton & Company, Inc.

Karen Horney studied narcissists before studying narcissists was cool, and she did it brilliantly. If you like a scientific approach, do start here.

Find the latest of what Alexandra Nouri has to say on the matter, at

http://alexandranouri.com/

Lying, deceiving, and manipulation are natural talents for psychopaths. When caught in a lie or challenged with the truth, they are seldom perplexed or embarrassed -- they simply change their stories or attempt to rework the facts so that they appear to be consistent with the lie. The results are a series of contradictory statements and a thoroughly confused listener.

--Robert Hare

When primitive aggression directly infiltrates the pathological grandiose self, we have what Kernberg calls "malignant narcissism." These patients experience triumph over inflicting fear and pain in others. Their self-esteem is enhanced when they experience sadistic pleasure.

--Desy Safan-Gerard, PhD

Q: How many narcissists does it take to screw in a lightbulb?

A: One. He holds the bulb and the world revolves around him.

I feel like I've finally taken the first true step. I now believe that he truly is a moron.

--E.P.

Tonight, when you lay your head on your pillow, forget how far you still have to go. Look instead at how far you've already come.

--Bob Moawad

Made in the USA
Middletown, DE
05 January 2018